DESTINATION

ROTOR

Jack Sprosen

The Bathhouse, today housing Rotorua's museum.

JENNY HAWORTH

VIKING

Jack Sprosen

The summit of Mount Tarawera — ripped apart by an eruption in 1886.

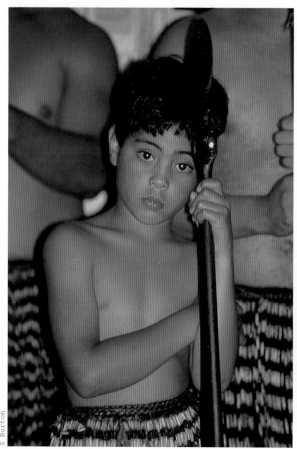

S Burton

A young performer.

Jack Sprosen

Poutukumanawa.

Boiling Cauldron

Mud pools.

Jack Sprosen

Lake Rotorua was created by a series of immense explosions, one of the largest occurring 142,000 years ago. During this explosion 200 cubic kilometres of magma was blown from the centre of the earth and the surface collapsed into a caldera, which eventually filled with water. The size of this explosion is difficult to imagine but one writer compares it to burying Auckland under two kilometres of ash.

Previous volcanic activity created the Mamaku Ranges and Lake Okataina, and later activity built Mount Ngongotaha, Mokoia Island, Hospital Hill and Kawaha Point.

Unlike Auckland, after a violent spate of land building, thermal activity did not die away. All around the city there are mud pools and fumaroles, and, just over a hundred years ago, Mount Tarawera erupted, burying villages, killing 150 people and destroying the famous Pink and White Terraces.

Rotorua's main geothermal field runs right under the inner city from Whakarewarewa to Ohinemutu and Kuirau Park. Businesses occasionally find thermal activity under their buildings — this has happened at the Rotorua Visitor's Centre. In the Government Gardens, steam from hot pools drifts across ducks swimming in the lagoon or lawn bowlers battling over a head. The smell of sulphur pervades the region.

Hotels and motels sink bores for private thermal pools and some home owners use steam for heating.

NEAR DISASTER

In the early 1980s, Rotorua learnt that its thermal reserves were not inexhaustible. By that time around 600 bores, some 120 metres deep, were drawing steam and hot water from the central geothermal field, and volcanic activity, particularly at Whakarewarewa, was seriously affected.

Before 1950 a dozen active geysers had drawn crowds to Whakarewarewa, but their activity was declining. Legislation closed down the private bores nearby, and this gave the geysers a new lease of life. ■

Whakarewarewa

Rahui Marae.

The village of Whakarewarewa is one of Rotorua's most active thermal areas, and includes some 500 hot springs, fumaroles and boiling mud pools. Visiting 'Whaka' is like walking through a safety valve for the earth's molten heart.

Most spectacular is the geyser field, particularly Pohutu, which erupts about 20 times a day to a height of three metres. The neighbouring Prince of Wales geyser bubbles for about 90 per cent of the day, but usually only to a height of two metres. Its behaviour indicates when Pohutu and nearby Waikorohihi will erupt.

Pohutu geyser.

Water from these geysers is rich in silica and, as it splashes across a rapidly growing terrace into the river, it has built a hanging cobweb reaching down from ledge to ledge.

The most famous of Whaka's mud pools is Ngamokaiakoko — the frog pool. Here the simmering mud jumps and plops like frogs leaping from the water. Activity varies according to the weather. After rain, the mud is more liquid and the 'frogs' jump furiously; in dry weather the thicker mud builds steep-sided cones and the 'frogs' revert to a slow, steady plop.

Whakarewarewa is controlled by the Ngati Tuhourangi people, who settled there after the Tarawera eruption destroyed their village at Te Wairoa. Many of their famous leaders, like Wi Keepa and Guide Sophia, the heroes of the Tarawera eruption, lie buried in vault-like graves alongside the track.

The thermal reserve is fringed on both sides by Maori villages. Next to the Arts and Crafts Centre is Rotowhio Pa. This serves both as a reconstruction of an ancient fortified pa as well as a modern ceremonial marae. The main building on the marae is Te Aronui-a-Rua, the meeting house. Its carving was the work of trainees at the Institute over a ten-year period and it is the centre for their programme of performing arts.

Also on the marae is an intricately carved pataka (storehouse) exhibited in the International South Seas Exhibition in Hagley Park, Christchurch, in 1906, and the Te-Ara-Wai war canoe carved by the Institute for the city's centennial celebrations in 1980. On special occasions it is fully decorated as a waka taua, and Maori warriors paddle it across Lake Rotorua.

On the other side of the reserve is Rahui where some families live in close proximity to the thermal pools which they use for cooking and for bathing. ■

Boiling mud.

The Pink and White Terraces

Hinemihi meeting house before Tarawera eruption (top); Te Wairoa before eruption.

I n the nineteenth century, visitors came from all over the world to see the Pink and White Terraces sited at Lake Rotomahana. These beautiful natural formations were so elaborate that many regarded them as the eighth wonder of the world.

Many paintings, photographs and descriptions were made of the terraces. Ferdinand von Hochstetter wrote of Te Tarata, the White Terrace: "It is as if a waterfall plunging over the steps had suddenly been transformed into stone."

Te Tarata rose from the shore of Lake Rotomahana to a height of 50 metres in a succession of steps, and covered three hectares. The white sinter glistened like alabaster and was shot with brilliant flashes of colour like an immense opal. Each terrace was hung with chalcedonic stalactites. At the top there was a crater of about 100 metres in diameter, from which blue boiling water bubbled and overflowed down the terraces.

Otukapuarangi, the Pink Terrace, rose more gently from the lake. Her terraced steps were wider and, according to Hochstetter, "prettier and finer in formation . . . [and] a soft rose red . . . invests the wonderful formation as if in a glow".

For James Inglis, a Scottish traveller, the real beauty of Otukapuarangi came from "a perpetual pattering of tiny cascades, ringing like silver bells . . . the hillside alive with the rush of pearls, diamonds and gems of refulgent lustre . . . the great circular basin at the top full to the brim with water, at boiling point, of the most exquisite blue".

Visitors on a day trip from Te Wairoa went first to the White Terrace, climbing the various terraces to see the thermal activity at the top. Here they ate lunch, much of which was cooked in the thermal pools.

Later they crossed to the Pink Terraces where they could bathe — first the women and then the men. The Europeans changed discreetly in the manuka. For warmer water the swimmers climbed higher up the terraces. As Inglis wrote of his thermal pool: "The floor seems made of pearly sago and a soft deposit covers the sides and bottom of the bathing pools . . . we roll lazily about in Sybaritic enjoyment". ■

Pink Terrace (Otukapuarangi) (top) and White Terrace (Te Tarata) as painted by Charles Blomfield (1848–1926).

Tarawera

Early in 1886 there were a number of disquieting signs. For the Maori the most ominous was the appearance of a phantom canoe late in May. A group of tourists led by Guide Sophia were crossing Lake Tarawera when suddenly, out of the mist, came a large waka taua — a war canoe. Manned by 12 paddlers, it shot past the travellers on its way to Mount Tarawera.

The Te Wairoa Maori realised none of their people were on board. The canoe was travelling at such speed towards their sacred burial mountain, Mount Tarawera, they knew it meant death.

Even the Europeans were worried — in the preceding months there had been an increasing number of earthquakes. Also the thermal areas were far more active, and at Lake Tarawera, on the same day as the phantom canoe, the water had surged backwards and forwards across the shoreline.

Lack of modern monitoring meant that no one knew where or when any great disturbance might occur. On 9 June, guests and residents at Te Wairoa went to bed only to be woken in the early hours of the morning by "vibrations and jolting". They found to their horror that Mt Tarawera was erupting.

Joseph McRae, the hotel owner, wrote: "The mountain had three craters and flames of fire were shooting up fully a thousand feet. There seemed to be a continuous shower of balls of fire for miles around." McRae and his guests took shelter in the hotel's smoking-room.

Later, McRae's brother-in-law, William Bird, recorded their plight: "An ominous sound near at hand drew our attention to the ceiling joists of our refuge, and we saw that they were sagging dangerously. Weakened by the weight of mud and the continuous earth tremors they were at the point of collapsing . . ." The

Burton Brothers 1886, Museum of NZ

Burton Brothers 1886, Museum of NZ

Te Wairoa after the eruption (top); and Rewiri outside a buried whare after the Tararewa eruption, June 1886.

Eruption

Museum of NZ

Burton Brothers 1886, Museum of NZ

Blythe and Lunds outside a buried building, Te Wairoa (top); and Sophia's whare where many sheltered.

party escaped to another room of the hotel, although one of them, an English tourist, Edwin Bainbridge, was killed when the room and verandah collapsed.

In this new room "we crouched in the darkness, deafened by the uproar, wondering how long the roof would hold under its increasing burden. To make matters worse, pungent sulphur fumes added their menace to the choking atmosphere and though the ceiling beams sagged downward more and more alarmingly, yet we could not imagine what fate awaited us if we left our shelter."

They remained in this room until it seemed likely to collapse, and finally made their way to Guide Sophia's whare, where many in the village had found refuge.

By morning the eruption had stopped but the countryside around was completely desolate. Joseph McRae wrote: "Every tree and green thing had been destroyed, and the bush road blocked up with mud and fallen timber. We returned to Wairoa and commenced to dig for the bodies of the Haszards" — Haszard had been the school teacher and his house was completely destroyed. Eventually Mrs Haszard was found alive but three of her five children were dead beside her.

Most of those who lost their lives were Maori, and the small villages like Te Ariki, which had been closer to the mountain, disappeared under a deep layer of ash and mud.

Of the beautiful Pink and White Terraces there was no sign. Part of the eruption had occurred at Lake Rotomahana where the whole lake bed had blown up and been greatly enlarged. There is little doubt that the terraces were destroyed, despite subsequent hopes that they might be excavated. ∎

Photos by Jenny Haworth

After the eruption, the people of Te Wairoa moved away; there was nothing to keep them there; the land was covered in mud and most houses were submerged.

The Buried Village

Since the 1930s, the site has gradually been excavated, and now hundreds come each year to glimpse life in the 1880s, frozen in time in the same way that the eruption of Vesuvius which covered Pompeii preserved Roman life in AD72.

Most obvious is the close relationship between Maori and Pakeha. Many small, very simple whares were within metres of the rather sizeable Rotomahana Hotel. From the mud-encrusted remains of china and molten silver it is obvious that those who stayed at the hotel were well looked after.

Whares belonging to both Maori and Pakeha, a blacksmith's forge and the remains of McRae's hotel have been uncovered. Many artefacts, covered with liquid mud during the eruption, are on display.

One of the few buildings left standing after the eruption was Hinemihi — the Maori meeting house. Many had sheltered here during the terrible night. After the village was abandoned, Hinemihi was bought by Lord Onslow (the Governor-General, 1889–1892) for £50. He took it back to his stately home, Clandon Park, Surrey, where for many years it was used as a boathouse. Now the property of the National Trust, the meeting house stands forlornly beside the splendid 18th-century house. ■

From top: Buried Village's pre-European stone house; the flour mill; Tuhoto Ariki's whare.

The crater, Mount Tarawera.

Peter Morath

Mount Tarawera

The summit of Mount Tarawera was ripped open by the 1886 eruption; along its three peaks runs a gash varying in depth from 90 to 270 metres and up to 2.5 metres wide. Standing on the edge of this immense crater one senses the awesome power of the eruption and the destruction it caused.

Today the craters are benign and those on trips climb around their edge and slide down an immense slope of scree, but the scars suggest how unpredictable the mountain is.

A four-wheel-drive track winds its way to the top of the mountain. Fit walkers can use this to walk up the mountain and explore the summit area. Others arrive by helicopter. ■

Warbrick Terrace, Waimangu.

Waimangu Valley Black Water

As if to compensate for the Tarawera eruption, nature created a thermal wonderland in the Waimangu Valley. Echo Crater was formed on 10 June 1886, but the valley's main attraction was the Waimangu Geyser, which between 1901 and 1904 belched black water to a height of 450 metres. It self-destructed in November 1904, during a spectacular eruption that is thought to have destroyed its underground plumbing. The geyser never bubbled again and now its site is dormant and covered with prostrate kanuka, a plant found only in thermal areas.

But eruptions continued in other parts of Echo Crater and after a particularly violent eruption in 1917, which blew up the accommodation house and killed two, the crater filled with water. This became known as Frying Pan Lake and is the largest hot spring in the world.

The neighbouring Inferno Crater was also formed

Frying Pan Lake and Cathedral Rocks, Waimangu.

in June 1886 as part of the Tarawera eruption. This crater follows a very unusual rhythmic 38-day cycle, overflowing and then refilling during that time.

A walking track runs around the edge of Frying Pan Lake, up to Inferno Crater, and then follows a warm stream with deposits of silica as it wends its way to Lake Rotomahana.

On the way down visitors pass numerous terraces, but the most spectacular of these is the Warbrick, which was named after a guide. It was formed when the level of the lake dropped to expose a ridge.

At the lake edge visitors take the boat *Ariki Moana* to see the Steaming Cliffs, an area of intense geothermal activity not far from what was the site of the Pink Terraces. The boat crosses the site of the White Terraces, now buried by the lake.

Above the whole area Mount Tarawera broods darkly. ■

Champagne Pool.

Waiotapu Sacred Water

Steam vent and sulphur deposit.

This geothermal field on the side of Maungakakaramea (Rainbow Mountain) is famous for its colours. The central feature of the reserve is the Champagne Pool — a fifth of a hectare of boiling water surrounded by a sinter rim stained a brilliant orange. Minerals found in the pool include gold, silver, mercury, sulphur, arsenic and thallium. These have stained the Artist's Palette in a brilliant kaleidoscope of yellow, orange, green, grey, black, red, purple and white. The colours constantly change as the deposits in the water alter.

Sulphur-saturated water runs from the Palette down over the Primrose Terrace, which descends in a series of tiny steps. It is the largest terrace of its type in New Zealand and is stained bright yellow because of the amount of sulphur in the water there.

The Lady Knox Geyser is a reliable performer. In 1896, prison labourers using its hot chloride water to wash their clothes found that the soap caused the spring to erupt. Blocks were placed around the vent and the Lady Knox continues to blow daily at 10.15 am, provided she receives her meal of soap. This disperses the upper layer of water and allows superheated steam and water to rush through the vent. ■

The old Rotorua Bathhouse and Government Gardens (top); and the Blue Baths and gardens.

Spa Centre

Last century, many people believed that bathing in thermal waters would cure illnesses such as rheumatism, insomnia, skin diseases and sexual impotence. Spa centres in Europe attracted Society, wealthy people who came to improve their health and join in an exciting round of cultural and social activities. Rotorua was heralded as the future Antipodean spa centre, drawing fashionable clientele from Australia and colonial Asia. To host these visitors, bathhouses were built and spacious gardens planted.

The most elegant building was the Rotorua Bathhouse, now the Museum of Art and History. It was designed with a gracious foyer, to serve as both a meeting place and a centre for treatment. In the upstairs gallery, an orchestra played daily during the Season, but in either wing, behind the closed doors, the invalids soaked in thermal waters, and were massaged and treated with primitive electrotherapy.

The lawn in front of the Bathhouse has altered little since 1900. The gardens, bowling greens and croquet lawns suggest the restful elegance of the Edwardian age, as do the 1900 band rotunda and Te Runanga, the teahouse, now re-opened after restoration.

For many years the gardens were surrounded by gracious hotels. Brents and the old Grand have disappeared, but the Prince's Gate remains. This has a highly decorated facade — two floors of wide balconies with beautifully carved balustrades. Inside, it has been carefully restored to reflect the style of the 1920s. The hotel originally stood in Waihi, but it was dismantled and removed to Rotorua in 1917. ■

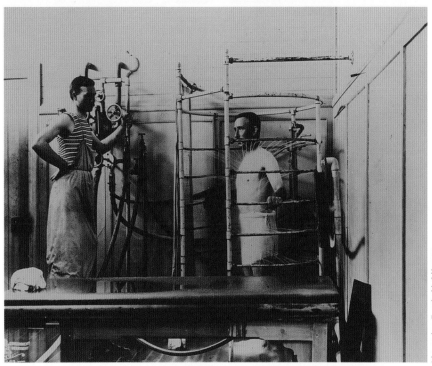

Early treatment at the Government Bathhouse.

Alexander Turnbull Library

Gareth Eyres

RELAXING ROTORUA

Jack Sprosen

Gareth Eyres

Tourism Rotorua

Tourism Rotorua

R *otorua is one of the North Island's more popular recreation centres. It caters for thrill-seekers as well as for those who simply want to relax or enjoy their favourite sport.* ∎

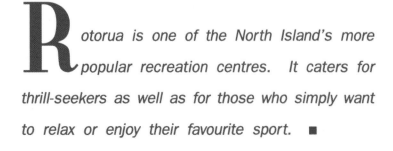

Clockwise: Relaxing in the Polynesian Pools; the pools; trout fishing; walking in the Redwoods, Whakarewarewa; golf; white-water rafting, Kaituna; kayaking.

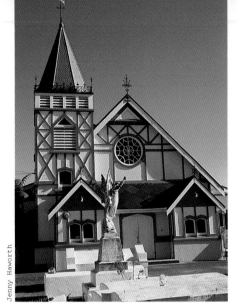

Jenny Haworth

St Faith's, Ohinemutu (left); and the
carved bust of Queen Victoria.

Te Arawa

Jack Sprosen

Most Maori who call Rotorua home claim descent from those who arrived on Te Arawa canoe, probably in the mid 14th century. They came from the legendary land of Hawaiki, somewhere in Eastern Polynesia. The Arawa people believe that Tamatekapua was the leader who brought them to Maketu in the Bay of Plenty. They have developed a whole series of legends about this chief and the voyage to New Zealand. These often feature in Maori concert recitals.

Ihenga, another young Arawa man, is credited with discovering Rotorua. Ihenga was out in the bush hunting for delicacies for his pregnant wife, when one of his dogs disappeared while chasing a kiwi. It returned sometime later with its coat wet and 'threw up' a meal of half-digested fish. Ihenga realised he was near water and he searched until he discovered Rotoiti, the small lake, and Rotorua, the second lake.

Te Arawa moved inland to settle in Rotorua and the Taupo–National Park area. Legend tells that it was through their tohunga, Ngatoroirangi, that geothermal warmth came from Hawaiki. He climbed Mount Tongariro and was so cold as he neared the summit that he called to his sisters Pupu and Hoata to send him warmth from Hawaiki. They obliged and fire burst from the ground at White Island, in the thermal district and at Tongariro. ■

Tamatekapua, the main meeting house, Ohinemutu; and (right) a Maori representation of Christ at St Faith's, Ohinemutu.

Jack Sprosen

Ohinemutu

Tourism Rotorua

Sited on the edge of Lake Rotorua, Ohinemutu has been the home of the Ngati Whakaue for hundreds of years. Before Rotorua was planned in the 1880s, Ohinemutu was where most of the visitors stayed.

Visitors are welcome to wander through the main marae, which is dominated by Tamatekapua, a whare runanga, which celebrates the captain of the Arawa canoe. The present building, where there are nightly concerts, was constructed just after World War II, but many of its carvings date from the mid 19th century.

Across the marae on the edge of the lake, is the Tudor styled St Faith's Church. It was constructed in 1910 and its interior is richly decorated with Maori motifs. The walls are covered with tukutuku panels and the pews elaborately carved. A window looking out over the lake shows a Maori Christ, in a traditional woven cloak, who appears to be walking on the water.

Around St Faith's there is a small raised graveyard — the thermal activity at Ohinemutu makes it impossible to place the dead underground. Close to the church are Maori and Pakeha who have been of great importance to Arawa people. Amongst them is Gilbert Mair, a Pakeha, who led Te Arawa in battles against Te Kooti, a famous Maori military leader and prophet. Behind, in lakeside graves, are members of the Maori Battalion who served overseas in two world wars.

On one side of the marae is a carved bust of Queen Victoria that was presented to Te Arawa out of gratitude for their loyalty during the New Zealand Wars.

Ohinemutu is one of the most historic maraes in the country and is a focus point in the area. Locals come to relax in the shade of Tamatekapua, to worship at St Faith's or to cook in one of the steaming vents. They welcome the procession of visitors and are willing to answer questions. ■

The Arts and Crafts Centre at Whakarewarewa

Photos by Jack Sprosen

Carver at work.

Weaving a piupiu.

This institute was established in 1963 to teach traditional Maori crafts, such as carving and weaving, that were in danger of being lost. Visitors watch craftspeople at work, and learn how the patterns and colours used in the traditional garments are created and the natural fibres are treated for use.

On the main carving floor, the master carvers and their apprentices work on carvings. Young Maori men come here for a three-year training course and learn not only about the carving traditions of their own iwi (tribe), but of all other iwi. They also study whakapapa — the genealogies which give them many of their subjects — the weapons and the traditional way of life.

Maori craftspeople show how the flax is patterned, stripped, dried and prepared so that piupiu, the skirt worn by concert parties, can be made. Just as their ancestors did, Maori still use the sharp edge of the mussel shell to strip the flax back to the fibre.

Others, there, demonstrate taniko weaving, showing how the brilliant coloured threads are patterned into bodices and bands. They explain just what dyes and natural fibres were used in the pre-Pakeha days. ■

Concert Parties

Maori concert groups perform nightly in Rotorua. These keep alive the tradition of welcoming guests with songs and dances. They include haka, poi dances, waiata and action songs as well as contemporary Maori music. Some relate the exploits of the ancestors like Tamatekapua or tell the love story of Tutanekai and Hinemoa. Often these concert programmes are adapted from what happens on a marae.

For those who want to see what happens on the marae, the full ceremonial welcome is performed at Tumunui and at Rakeiao Marae near Lake Rotoiti.

First the hosts have to be sure that the guests have come in peace and so a wero (challenge) is issued by a Maori warrior swinging a taiaha. When the newcomers accept the challenge as friends, they are welcomed with a powhiri — a series of speeches and waiata which draws the visitors across the marae, until they join in a hongi. This is where the hosts and guests press noses and share each others breath as a symbol of togetherness.

This ceremony usually takes place in front of, or just inside, the main meeting house. The guests' arrival is then celebrated with further haka, poi dances and action songs, and then, as members of one family, the guests share a hangi. ■

Maori concert, Rakeiao Marae.

Hangi

Like many Polynesians, the Maori cooked food in underground ovens. A pit was dug and lined with heavy stones, upon which a fire was lit. Once the stones were hot, the fire was dampened down with water and leaves, often fern fronds. Baskets of food were placed in the oven, covered with leaves and mats, and earth was heaped on top to seal in the steam.

Te Arawa people used natural steam. Food was placed in boxes in the thermal pools and the hot steam gradually cooked it. Nowadays most of the hangi served to guests in hotels are cooked in a steam box.

Food from an earth hangi has a much stronger flavour — there is a definite smoky taste — whereas the food from a steam hangi has a gentler blend of flavours. ■

Opening the hangi, Rakeiao Marae.

Tourism Rotorua

Geoff Moon

The city of Rotorua is the centre of the North Island lake district — 11 major lakes are within easy reach of the city. Each has its own charm. Some are ringed with houses and holiday baches, while others, like Okataina, Tikitapu and Rotomahana, are nature reserves.

The Lakes

LAKE ROTORUA

Parts of the foreshore are suburban, but elsewhere there are wildlife refuges and walking tracks.

The foreshore bordering the Government Gardens is a wildlife sanctuary. It is a major nesting area for the protected red- and black-billed gulls. A walking track leads from the Bathhouse around Motutara Point, the main site of the sanctuary, and back to the wharf, where boats depart on lake cruises.

The gem of Lake Rotorua is Mokoia Island. It has special significance for Te Arawa and for many years much of it was tapu. Visitors can now spend a day there, catching a boat from the jetty to picnic by Hinemoa's Pool and climb to the summit of the island. ∎

Peter Morath

Opposite page: The Lakeland Queen (top); and (below) Mokoia Island, Lake Rotorua. Left: Lake Rotorua at dawn. Below: Lake Rotorua.

Hinemoa and Tutanekai

The legend of these lovers is one of the most beautiful in Maoridom.

Tutanekai, the son of Whakaue-Kaipapa, paramount chief of Te Arawa, lived on Mokoia Island. He and his brothers went to a hui across the lake, where they saw the beautiful Hinemoa, the daughter of the chief of the Tuhourangi. All the brothers fell in love with her, but she favoured Tutanekai.

He encouraged Hinemoa to follow him, telling her that when she heard him play his flute she was to slip out of her village, take a canoe and paddle to Mokoia. But Hinemoa, although she frequently heard the flute calling her, found it impossible to escape her guardians.

One night Hinemoa managed to slip out, but when she arrived at the water's edge she found that all the canoes had been drawn up on high ground. They were too heavy for her to haul into the water, so she decided to swim out to the island.

She tied two gourds around her waist for buoyancy and dived into the water. Tutanekai's music guided her towards the island.

By the time she arrived, he had stopped playing. She was exhausted after the long swim and rested her tired feet in the warm pool on Mokoia.

Tutanekai's servant came to draw water from a nearby spring; Hinemoa seized his gourd and broke it. She did this several times before Tutanekai came rushing out to

see who was breaking the gourds. He instantly recognised Hinemoa.

Legend suggests that they spent the night together and when Tutanekai failed to appear next the morning his father sent a servant to find the son. He peeped in the wharepuni and found two pairs of feet, not one, under the sleeping mat. He rushed to tell Whakaue and a marriage feast was hastily arranged. ■

Jack Sprosen

Lakes Rotorua and Rotoiti linked by the Ohau Channel (top); and lakeshore boatsheds, Lake Rotoiti.

David Gray, Focus New Zealand

LAKE ROTOITI

Rotoiti is very popular with locals and visitors for trout fishing, boating and sailing. It is rich in Maori history. At one end is Hongi's Track, so called because it is said to be the route Hongi Hika, the Northland Nga Puhi chief, used when he came to attack Te Arawa in 1823.

The centrepiece of the track is the Hinehopu tree — a wishing tree. The Uru-uru-whenua ceremony, in which a coin or fern frond is placed in the tree, is said to help the traveller enjoy favourable weather.

A walking track through the bush runs parallel to the road. This is part of a gift from the Ngati Pikiao to the Crown. ■

OKERE FALLS

The Kaituna River plunges through a rocky gorge in a series of leaps. The most spectacular drop is over the Okere Falls, which has become the ultimate test for whitewater rafters.

A narrow staircase, Hinemoa's Steps, gives walkers access to the falls. It was chipped out of the cliff face early this century. ■

Jack Sprosen

Lake Okataina.

LAKE OKATAINA

This is the scenic gem of Rotorua. The lake is surrounded by bush and its clear sparkling waters and pumice beaches make it a great favourite with those who want to relax. The lake and surrounding bush, an area of 4,388 hectares, is a scenic reserve, presented to the people of New Zealand by the Ngati Tarawhai people.

The reserve is laced with walking tracks. Short tracks run from the access road to the lake. One of the most beautiful takes you to the isolated crater lakes, like Rotoatua, lost in the bush.

Longer tracks include the Eastern Okataina walkway. This is an easy-graded track around the eastern side of the lake. It takes about two-and-a-half hours to reach the top of the lake and another half-hour to cross the divide to Lake Tarawera.

Turn off from this walkway to visit Te Koutu Point — one of the most important pre-European pa on the edge of the lake. The headland is terraced and honeycombed with some 45 food storage pits (rua).

Another superb walk follows the western shoreline, along a pumice beach for most of the way, although occasionally you wade into the shallow water to edge around a headland. Very quickly you are on your own with only birds and butterflies for company. ■

LAKE TIKITAPU
The Blue Lake

Tikitapu is perhaps the best lake for swimming and canoeing near Rotorua. It is surrounded by a thick bush with many ferns, which comes right to the edge of the lake. A walking track circles the shore. ■

LAKE ROTOKAKAHI
The Green Lake

Although adjacent to Tikitapu, this lake is a quite distinctive shade of green. Rotokakahi is sacred to the Ngati Tuhourangi, whose burial ground is on an island in the centre of the lake. This makes the lake tapu, and so no one can swim, fish or boat here, although its foreshore is open to walkers. ■

Jack Sprosen

Lake Tikitapu (top); and Lake Rotokakahi.

LAKE TARAWERA

The mountain is an awe-inspiring backdrop — in front the lake is placid and picturesque. Only a small proportion of Lake Tarawera is open by access road, so it is very quiet. ■

Jenny Haworth

Lake Tarawera (right), with Mount Tarawera as a backdrop; Lake Okareka (bottom right) with Lake Tarawera in the background.

Gaylene Earl, Focus New Zealand

Jack Sprosen

Trout Fishing

Trout fishing in the Ohau Channel between Lake Rotorua and Lake Rotoiti.

Jack Sprosen

Rainbow is the most common species of trout caught in the Rotorua district, although brown trout and brook char can also be hooked.

The rainbow is a particularly sleek, athletic fish, recognised as a good fighter. They are quite distinctive with their bright strip of colour — a blend of red, reddish orange and magenta — that runs from the gill cover to the anal fin.

Rainbow trout were introduced into New Zealand from Sonoma County in California in 1883. Then, they were an ocean fish which came up the rivers to spawn, but the local trout have adapted well to lake-streamlet conditions.

Lake Rotorua is fed by a number of spawning streams, which are so productive that there is no need to release surplus fingerlings from the hatchery into the lake. Rotorua is open to anglers all year, but the tributary streams close from 1 July to 30 November.

Tourism Rotorua

A rainbow trout.

Trout fishing in New Zealand is a sport and all fisher people have to have a licence and approved tackle. There are daily bag limits and minimum sizes for the fish caught. No trout can be sold or served in restaurants — if you want to eat trout you have to catch them.

Numerous companies offer fishing packages. These include all equipment, transport, licences and advice on how and where to try your luck. ■

Trout pool at Rainbow Springs.

Andris Apse

Rainbow and Fairy Springs

In the fern-fringed ponds trout — some of them an incredible size — zip and twist their way through the water. Offer them food and they jump and spin just as they do when hunting a fly. Many of the fish swimming in these pools are not captive but free to come and go from the lake. In season, they spawn in Waiowhiro Stream, a part of the complex.

Here you learn about the various types of trout and their characteristics. A mirror in the bed of one pool allows you to look at the underside of the fish; in another you can see beneath the water. Fish look the visitors straight in the eye, while they gaze in amazement at the size of individual fish.

The Springs, since they first opened to the public in 1931, have gradually developed into a wide-ranging flora and fauna park. Here endangered birds like kiwi, kea, kereru, kaka and morepork are on display, as is the tuatara, a New Zealand native reptile, whose breed is unchanged from the time of the dinosaurs.

Across the road is the Rainbow Farm Show. This involves visitors in the annual round of events on a mixed farm. Activities like milking cows, mustering and shearing sheep and feeding the lambs take place in paddocks and sheds that are part of the complex. ■

The Rainbow Farm Show.

Tourism Rotorua

The Agrodome

Photos by Tony Hadlow

T he Agrodome presents New Zealand farm life on stage. The main performers are the animals who have been carefully tutored and enjoy their roles. The commentary comes from a black-singletted farmer.

First 19 rams, each a different breed, tread the boards; they run up onto display rostra. Each has an exotic name; amongst them are Rugby the Drysdale, Major the Hampshire, and Winston the English Leicester. The farmer's job is to describe the breed and the breed's main characteristics.

Dogs then bound in. Two huntaways leap around but respond quickly to a single whistle, running over the backs of the rams to pose for cameras.

Next comes the strong-eyed dog, who musters by gazing silently and fixedly at his quarry — he organises two geese around the stage.

The commentator has to have all the skills of the local farmer. He has to work the sheep dogs, shear a heavy fleeced sheep, run an auction and teach the audience how to milk a cow and feed lambs.

The strength of the show is that it is never gimmicky. It makes good use of the animals in a natural way while providing an insight into the methods and problems of the local industry. For many it will be the first time they have been able to have their photographs taken with these animals.

Afterwards there is a chance to explore New Zealand farm life. Surrounding the Agrodome is a 160-hectare farm. Visitors catch the farm tour bus and learn how kiwifruit are grown, sample natural honey straight from the hives and study methods used to farm sheep, goats, deer and cattle. There is even a chance to try clay-pigeon shooting. ■

Taonga, Nukuteatiati — porch figure.

Arawa taonga, Poutukumanawa.

Photos by Jack Sprosen

Museum of Art and History

(Te Whare Taonga o Te Arawa)

For many years the Rotorua Bathhouse lay derelict and was in danger of being demolished. Ownership was transferred to the Rotorua City Council in 1963 and it has been used as an art and history museum in such a way that much of the character of the old building has survived.

The south wing houses the tribal treasures of Te Arawa. A permanent exhibition 'Te Ohaaki o Houmaitawhiti', tells the story of these people, illustrated through their taonga (treasures), each of which encompasses the spiritual mauri of the people. On display are some of the great carvings, weapons, greenstone pieces and intricately woven feather cloaks owned collectively by Te Arawa people. Some of the pieces on display date back to pre-European times. Each taonga is an art work, contributes to tribal history and has its own special mauri (spirit).

For instance one group of Pouwhakarae are portraits of early Te Arawa ancestors. They were at the top of some of the palisade posts which once protected the main pa of Ngati Whakaue. Each of these carved ancestors was created to not only physically defend the people but also to act as a spiritual guardian. Say the Maori: "They are alive, they are watching, they are listening . . .".

In the north wing there is a detailed display on the Pink and White Terraces, the 1886 Tarawera eruption and the destruction of Te Wairoa village. The whole event is captured through vivid audio-visuals based on the accounts of those who survived the experience and the amazingly clear photographs of the Burton Brothers and Charles Spencer. There are few eruptions, until later this century, that have been so clearly documented.

Other galleries are used for a variety of exhibitions and often feature talented New Zealand artists, photographers and craftspeople, or focus on aspects of New Zealand history. ∎

Brian Moorhead, Focus New Zealand

Skyline gondola (top); and coming down the luge.

Raewyn Saville